Dedicated to My Children
who inspire me in ways I could never describe,
And their Mom who speaks my language.

SNOOT

(SNEWT) *v* :
To suck in rather than blow out
when blowing your nose.

WHYAHRHEA

(WHY-uh-REE-uh) *n* :
An inquisitive toddler's chain of
questions rattled off in rapid-fire
succession.

KIDDLES

(KID-duhls) *n* :
Crumbs and debris found in the
creases of your car's upholstery
when you remove a child's car seat.

YUPPING

(YUH-ping) *v* :
The act of acknowledging what your two-year-old is communicating to you when you have no idea what they're trying to say.

MISTORICAL PERSPECTIVE

(miss-TOHR-ick-uhl per-SPEC-tiv) *v* : Recollections of one's youth told to their children, which conveniently omit any and all immoral or illegal acts.

MOISTRATION

(moy-STRAY-shun) *n* :
The nauseous feeling that washes over you
when you're eating leftover food off your
kid's plate and realize that the piece you just
put in your mouth has already been chewed.

CURDLER

(KERD-luhr) *n* :
A sippy cup with milk in it that's been lost under a piece of furniture for several weeks.

CLANDES-DINE

(klan-DESS-dyne) *v* :

To hide from one's child while eating a cookie
so they don't ask for one too.

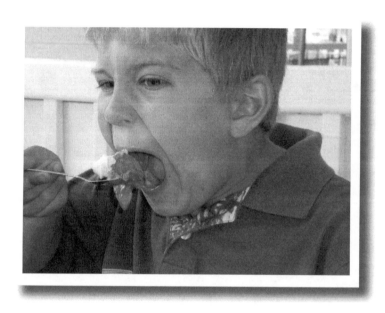

FULLISH

(FUL-ish) *adj* :
Too full to eat more carrots, yet fully prepared
to consume an ice cream sundae.

INVISIBOOBOO

(in-VIZ-uh-boo-boo) *n* :
The site on a child's body where you
unnecessarily applied a bandage to appease
them when they got hurt, though did not bleed.

DOVE CRY

(duv cry) *v* :

The sudden, emphatic and immediate need for a towel that overcomes a child when soap gets in their eyes.

(also referred to as: DIAL 911)

TRASHCANNAISSANCE MISSION

(trash-CAN-uh-sintz MISH-uhn) *n* :
Routine exercise of retrieving important items from the garbage that your toddlers threw away for fun.

(ie - silverware, TV remote, car keys)

HEINZ THEOREM

(Heinz THEE-ruhm) *n* :
Volume ratio of a toddler's ketchup that made it into his mouth divided by the amount contained on his clothes.

HOPPSPUCKER

(HOPS-pucker) *n* :
Reaction on a child's face to their first sip of beer.

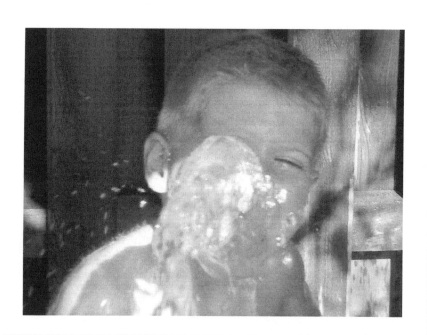

NOCTHIRSTAL

(nahk-THUR-stuhl) *n* :

A child's need for a bedside glass of water that they never drink from, but frequently spill.

N.R.A-DOLESENCE

(n.r.A-doh-LESS-entz) *n* :
The period when (predominantly male) children discover the playtime fun associated with pretending to kill people.

CRYDENTITY CRISIS

(cry-DENT-it-tee CRY-siss) *n* :
Silence that falls over a group of parents at a
playdate when a cry is heard in another room
and they are trying to determine if the crying
child is their's.

FLOORMET

(floor-MAY) *n* :

An adult who has no quarrel eating and enjoying food their child has rejected and thrown on the ground.

THREEMAGEDDON

(THREE-muh-ged-dun) *n* :
The supposed hellfire and brimstone that would erupt should an annoyed mother reach the third digit while counting aloud to 3 when prompting a child to get his act together...
"ONE... TWOOOOOO!!!!!!!!! ..."

INFLAGING

(inn-FLAY-jing) *v* :
When a 4-year-old insists that she is 6.

ORTHODONTREPRENEUR

(orth-o-DAHN-truh-pren-orr) *n* :
A child who wants to knock all of his own teeth
out in the interest of a hefty payday from the
Tooth Fairy.

THREEQUELS

(THREE-kwelz) *n* :

The three books you read to your kids AFTER you read them "the last book" before bed.

CRAYOFF

(CRAY-off) *v* :

To mark outside of the lines in a coloring book.

SLEDENTARY

(SLED-en-tehr-ee) *adj* :
A child's state of being so bundled up to face
the winter elements that they cannot move.

OREOSIS

(or-ee-OH-siss) *n* :
The insatiable hunger for desserts.

DISDRESS

(diss-DRESS) *n* :
The unfashionable looks achieved by toddlers
who are just learning to dress themselves.
(also *adj* : "In Disdress")

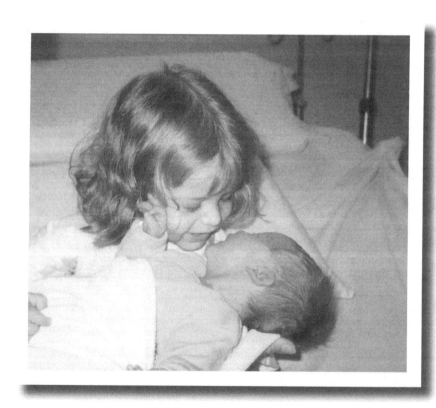

RESEMBULLATE

(re-ZEM-bull-ayt) *v* :

To assess which parent a newborn baby looks like.
(When really they all look like E.T.)

TOONED OUT

(TOOND out) *adj* :
Catatonic state of a child seated before
a television.

FECALARITY

(fee-cull-AYR-itt-ee) *n* :
The comic force which causes a child to
laugh himself to the floor at the mere
mention of the word "poop."

DADUATION

(DAD-ju-AY-shun) *n* :

The painful realization that you are quickly and irreversibly turning into your parents.

SHOTTUP

(shod-UP) *v* :

To neglect to mention to your children that their visit to the doctor will yield not only a sticker and a lollipop, but also a sharp needle jabbed in their arm.

MONOPOLOOZE

(mon-NAH-puh-looz) *v* :
To strategically lose a board game against an
unsportsmanlike child.

REGURGITIGHTEN

(re-GUHR-jih-tie-tuhn) *v* :
To brace yourself upon ascertaining that your ill child is about to barf on you.

SANDSWITCH

(SAN-swich) *v* :
A kindergartener's 11th hour decision to change his mind about what he wants you to pack him for lunch.

MISCROSS

(miss-CROSS) *v* :
A child's failure to take the precaution of looking both ways until they're in the middle of the street.

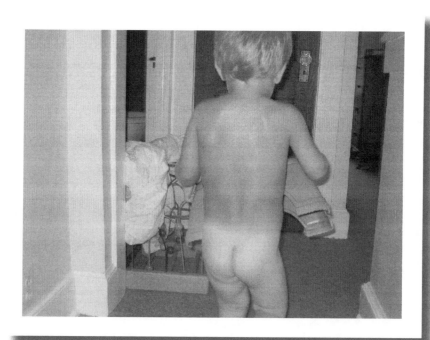

ASSIBITION

(ASS-uh-bish-uhn) *n* :
Immodest stage during which young boys see nothing wrong with taking their pants down to their ankles to pee in a public restroom.

KEGULATE

(KEG-u-layt) *v* :
To ponder the future cost of your child's
college education while recollecting that
mostly what you did there was drink beer.

ETHIOPULENCE

(EETH-ee-O-pew-lentz) *adj* :

State of good fortune neglected by every child with a roof over their head and food to eat.

ie-

Parent: "Do you know how lucky you are to have a roof over your head and food to eat?"

Child: "Do you know that Jake has X-Box!?"

KINDERWARP

(KIN-duhr-worp) *n* :
A child's time-management logic by which
he thinks he can watch a movie, play a video
game and have hot chocolate because bedtime
is 8 o'clock and it's only 7:53.

KODICK

(COH-dik) *n* :

The one child who refuses to cooperate in the taking of a family photograph.

OVEREXPOSURES

(O-vuhr-eck-SPOH-zuhrs) *n* :
The 80-or-so hours of unwatchably boring footage
you'll shoot during the first 3 months of your first
child's life.

LINGUISTETS

(lin-GWISS-tetz) *n* :
A child's mispronunciations of words left uncorrected by parents who find them cute or funny. (ie - "Peckeroni Pizza")

SCOOBUNGLE

(skoo-BUNG-uhl) *v* :
To prematurely bite off the bottom tip of an ice cream cone on a hot summer day.

SPITSICLE

(SPIT-sik-uhl) *n* :
The string of drool that extends from a baby's
mouth to his pants.

IMPOLERT

(im-poh-LURT) *n* :
A child's indiscreet public call of attention
to a stranger's physical abnormality.
(ie - "He's only got ONE LEG!!!!")

NEWTON'S EXCEPTION

(NEW-tuhn's eck-SEP-shun) *n* : The explanation to one's child that a helium balloon lost outside is never coming back.

CHARMANGLED

(shar-MANG-eld) *adj* :
The discombobulated state of a roll of toilet paper
that's been unfurled and recoiled several times
by toddlers who liken this bathroom accessory
to a party favor.

DISHEART-TO-HEART TALK

(diss-HART-too-HART TAWK) *adj* :
Disappointing responses to your sincerest
proclamations of love for your children.
Dad: "I will love you and protect you forever
and ever my sweetest little princess."
Daughter (age 3): "Daddy, you have hair in your nose!"

DISROBIENTATION

(diss-ROE-bee-uhn-TAY-shun) *v* :
The pre-bathtime act of intentionally leaving
your toddler's half-removed shirt over their face
to distract them so you can more easily remove
their pants.

A.M. FREEZE

(A.M. freez) *v* :
The early morning hope, upon hearing a stirring infant or toddler, that if you stay perfectly still and quiet they will go back to sleep. (Never in the history of parenting has this worked.)

REWHINE

(REE-whyne) *n* :
The short light whine that a child emits immediately after you scold them to "Stop whining!"

RIDISCIPLINE

(rid-DISS-uh-plinn) *v* :

To make a preposterously empty threat.

ie -

"If you don't stop that right now, no more air!"

BLUFFANANCE

(BLUFF-uh-nentz) *n* :
The precise moment at which your idle
threats become completely ineffective
on your children.

WETSOXITY

(whet-SOX-itt-ee) *n* :
The magnetic-like force that draws children
not wearing boots into puddles.

BROFITTI

(bro-FEE-tee) *v* :

To scribble with permanent magic marker on the face of a younger sibling.

CHORUS ILLUS

(KOR-iss ILL-iss) (Latin) *adj* :
The decidedly unmelodic pitch of 50
preschool children singing at once.

CHINA SYNDROME

(CHY-nuh SIN-drohm) *n* :
The inexplicably dire necessity to drink only
from one particular cup or to eat only from one
particular plate.

NAPFUSION

(napp-FYOO-zhun) *n* :
The dilemma - to wake or not to wake a toddler
who falls asleep at 4 o'clock in the afternoon.

LULLACRY

(LULL-uh-cry) *n* :
The dramatic pause between a child's
sustaining an injury and beginning to wail.

DRINKLE

(DRING-kuhl) *n* :
The liquid burst emitted from the little straw
when a toddler grasps his juice box too tightly.
(also DRINKLER *n* :
a child prone to causing such liquid bursts.)

SPOONAMI

(spoo-NAH-mee) *n* :

The aftermath in your silverware drawer subsequent to letting your 3-year-old empty the dishwasher cutlery basket.

JEMIMA CLAUSE

(jeh-MY-muh clauz) *n* :
Leniency in the dietary code that allows
chocolate chip pancakes smothered in syrup and
whipped cream to be classified as "breakfast."

PAMPERATIONS

(pahm-per-AY-shuns) *n* :
The twisting, squirming and kicking a baby performs to make changing their diaper as difficult as possible.

LIBRIDO

(lib-REE-doh) *n* :

A man's disdain for literature about parenting.

DISSCRIPT

(diss-KRYPT) *v* :

To flub one's single line in a kindergarten play.

DEFRAMATION

(DEF-ruh-MAY-shun) *n* :
The sharp decline in photos and video taken of your second child relative to the amount taken of your first.

STONEWAIL

(STOWN-weyl) *v* :
The strategic act of displaying no emotion in response to your child's public tantrum.

WISHJACK

(WISH-jak) *v* :

To maliciously blow out the candles on another child's birthday cake.

NINTENDOID

(nin-TEN-doyd) *n* :

A child who is helplessly addicted to video games.
One who'd likely choose a video game over a
glass of water if he were in the middle of the
Mojave Desert at noon, even if he were on fire.

SHKOFF

(SHKAHF) *v* :

To remove one's shoes without first
untying the laces.

BUFFERT

(BUFF-uhrt) *n* :
The distance a child at the dinner table
insists on maintaining between himself
and a plate of food he does not wish to eat.

WANTIZONTAL

(WAHN-tiz-AHN-til) *adj* :
To be lying on the floor, body stiffened and
screaming at the top of one's lungs because you
did not get your way.

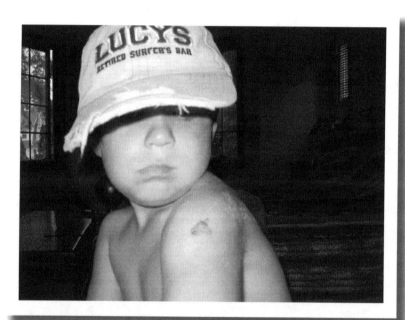

VACCINEMINEM

(VAK-sin-EM-in-NEM) *n* :
The candy reward given to a child for being brave
while getting his shots. (And even, frequently,
when they're not-so-brave.)

DISSLACKSIA

(diss-LAKS-ee-uh) *n* :
A young girl's insistence that she always wear
a dress.

KEDTUSIONS

(kedd-TOO-zhunz) *n* :
Kicks to the face sustained while trying to
tie a toddler's shoes.

TANGLET

(TANG-lett) *n* :

An impossibly complex knot created by a child in the early stages of learning to tie his shoes.

NIGHTCAPPETITE

(nite-CAPP-uh-tyte) *n* :
The "sudden hunger" portion of a child's
bedtime procrastination ritual.

OVERBUB

(O-vuhr-bubb) *v* :

To dispense five full pumps of liquid soap to wash two itty-bitty hands.

POLUTENESS

(poh-LOOT-ness) *n* :
A child's ability to say "please", "thank you"
and/or "I'm sorry" without the slightest trace
of sincerity.

KNICKKNOCK

(NIK-nok) *v* :

To riddle a grownup for extended periods of time with impossibly inane Knock-Knock jokes.

JEZEBUCK

(JEZZ-uh-buck) *n* :
A toddler who peels off his clothes at
inappropriate venues, such as a stuffy,
ornate religious celebration.

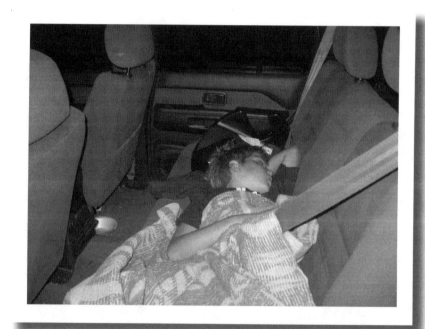

TRANSPORTOT

(TRANZ-poor-TAHT) *v* :
To carry a sleeping child from the car
to their bed without awakening them.

SILLABUSTER

(SILL-uh-BUSS-tuhr) *n* :
A child who recently learned to talk and feels
the need to do so continuously for hours with
little or no effort to make any kind of sense.

FARFER

(FARR-fuhr) *n* :
The half-terrified half-exhilarated squeal a
5-year-old girl emits while being kissed by
her grandfather.

SHITISTICS

(shih-TISS-tiks) *n* :
The incredibly inaccurate stats spouted
 by an 8-year-old boy while he watches a
sporting event.

FLOORCLOSE

(flor-CLOZ) *v* :

To obstruct a family room's main thoroughfare with a shoddily-constructed tower of blocks.

WICH HUNTER

(WICH HUHN-tuhr) *n* :

A child with a deep distaste for bread crusts.

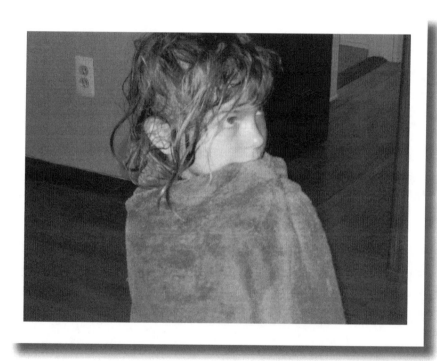

THUMBLE

(THUM-bull) *v* :
To speak incoherently with one's fingers in their mouth.

acknowledgments:
Getting this book off the ground was no small chore and I offer sincere thanks to everyone who helped me, encouraged me and tolerated me throughout the process. To name a few - My wife Kara, my wonderful children, my friends: Erl and Beth Rome, Jon Mace, Lisa Calanni for design ideas, Jon and Heather Whelan, Margaret Noonan and Michael Tatlow. And, as ever, my Mom and Dad and Brothers who never ridiculed me for thinking differently. Or haven't recently. At least not to my face. Thank you also to the photogenic individuals who so graciously appear in The KidDictionary photographs.

For more of this sort of nonsense, visit:
www.TheKidDictionary.com

Creator, Eric Ruhalter studied Economics at Dickinson College where he learned, first and foremost, that he's not the least bit interested in the theories and principles of Economics. So rather than study he began spending most of his time writing. Don't tell his father.

Made in the USA